Yellowstone National Park

Janet Piehl

Lerner Publications Company
Minneapolis

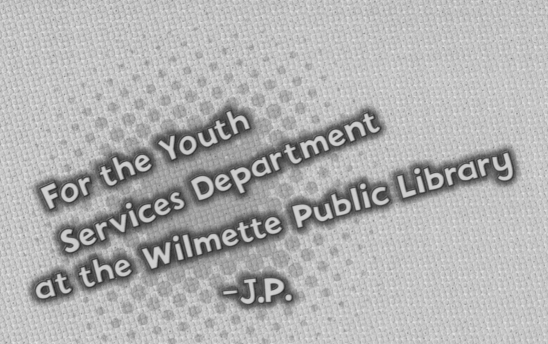

For the Youth
Services Department
at the Wilmette Public Library
–J.P.

Lerner Publications Company
A division of Lerner Publishing Group, Inc.
241 First Avenue North
Minneapolis, MN 55401 U.S.A.

Website address: www.lernerbooks.com

Library of Congress Cataloging-in-Publication Data

Piehl, Janet.
    Yellowstone National Park / by Janet Piehl.
        p.   cm. — (Lightning bolt books™—Famous places)
    Includes index.
    ISBN 978-0-7613-4455-1 (lib. bdg. : alk. paper)
    1. Yellowstone National Park—Juvenile literature. I. Title.
    F722.P54 2010
    978.752—dc22   2009020343

Manufactured in the United States of America
1 — BP — 12/15/09

Contents

Welcome to Yellowstone National Park ... page 4

Natural Wonders ... page 7

Becoming a National Park ... page 12

Yellowstone's Riches ... page 16

Amazing Recovery ... page 24

Map ... page 28

Fun Facts ... page 29

Glossary ... page 30

Further Reading ... page 31

Index ... page 32

Welcome to Yellowstone National Park

Where do bison, elk, and bears live? Where can you find towering mountains and black cliffs? And boiling-hot water shooting into the air?

These wonders and more are in Yellowstone National Park.

Boiling water and steam shoot out of the ground in Yellowstone National Park.

Yellowstone is in the western United States. Most of the park is in Wyoming. People from all around the world visit Yellowstone.

Natural Wonders

Why are there so many natural wonders in Yellowstone? A volcano made many of them. It erupted many times. There was a huge eruption 600,000 years ago.

This volcano erupted in Italy in 2002. Long ago, there was a huge eruption in Yellowstone.

Hot ash, lava, and rock shot out of the volcano.

The hot mix piled up on the ground. The piles hardened. They became mountains and rocks.

Smoke and ash pour out of this volcano in Russia.

Hot, melted rock still boils under the earth in Yellowstone. The melted rock heats water deep under the ground.

The hot, melted rock beneath the ground in Yellowstone heats the water in this spring. People swim in the warm water—even in winter!

The water comes up to Earth's surface sometimes. It even shoots into the air. This is a geyser. Other times, the water bubbles in a hot spring.

Bison stay warm in the winter near a hot spring. Yellowstone has more geysers and hot springs than anywhere else on Earth.

A volcano isn't the only thing that shaped Yellowstone. Glaciers helped form the park too. Glaciers are thick, moving sheets of ice. They cut holes in the ground. The holes become canyons, rivers, and lakes.

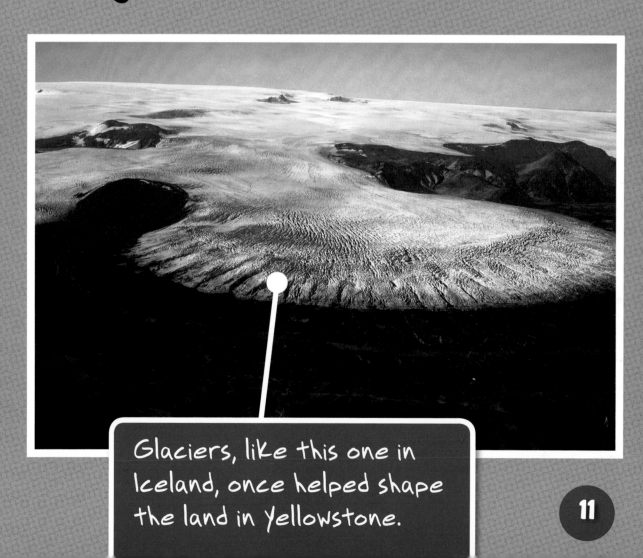

Glaciers, like this one in Iceland, once helped shape the land in Yellowstone.

Becoming a National Park

People have been in Yellowstone for more than eleven thousand years. Native Americans were the first to live there.

This stone tool was made by the Native Americans who first lived in Yellowstone.

In 1807, an explorer named John Colter became the first European American to see Yellowstone.

An actor plays the part of John Colter, in a history festival.

Soon more people came to the area. They saw that it was special. They wanted to keep it safe. In 1872, the U.S. government made Yellowstone the world's first national park.

U.S. president Teddy Roosevelt visited Yellowstone in 1903.

"FOR THE BENEFIT AND
ENJOYMENT OF THE PEOPLE"

YELLOWSTONE
NATIONAL
PARK

CREATED BY
ACT OF CONGRESS
MARCH 1, 1872

The U.S. government runs the park. The park's plants, animals, and land are protected. Anyone can enjoy Yellowstone's beauty.

15

Yellowstone's Riches

Yellowstone's best known site is Old Faithful. **This is the park's most famous geyser. Old Faithful shoots boiling water 130 feet (40 meters) into the air. This happens about every ninety minutes.**

Mammoth Hot Springs is another well-known site. It looks like a colorful waterfall. Water flows over rocks that look like steps.

Rocks form interesting shapes at Mammoth Hot Springs.

Have you ever seen stone trees? You can see them in Yellowstone! Volcanic ash buried whole forests millions of years ago. The trees turned to stone.

Volcanic ash turned this tree to stone.

A volcano also formed Obsidian Cliff. Hot lava flowed from the volcano. It cooled to form the black glass cliff.

Obsidian is a glass volcanic rock. If you look at it closely, you can see its dark color.

The Yellowstone
River flows into
Yellowstone Lake.
It rushes down
two tall waterfalls.
Then the river
passes through
Yellowstone's
Grand Canyon.

Water from the Yellowstone River pours over the Lower Falls into the Grand Canyon of Yellowstone.

Yellowstone also has mountains. Eagle Peak is Yellowstone's tallest mountain.

Yellowstone's Eagle Peak reaches into the bright blue sky.

Yellowstone is home to grizzly bears, deer, bighorn sheep, and cougars. Some wolves live there too. Swans, herons, pelicans, and eagles fly above.

Many kinds of flowers grow
in Yellowstone's meadows.
Evergreen trees grow in its forests.

Pink flowers called prairie
smoke add dabs of color to
a meadow in Yellowstone.

Amazing Recovery

In 1988, Yellowstone's forests were almost destroyed. Huge fires burned there. Animals lost their homes. Visitors left the park.

Smoke from the fires in Yellowstone billows from the forest.

But soon, the flowers, grasses, and forests grew back. Animals and people returned.

Grasses and wildflowers were the first plants to return to the forests of Yellowstone after the fires.

Visitors enjoy hiking, boating, and camping in Yellowstone. They watch the geysers and hot springs. And they look at the black cliffs, stone trees, and waterfalls.

What would you like to do in Yellowstone National Park?

Wooden walkways allow visitors to see some of Yellowstone's amazing sights up close.

Yellowstone National Park Area

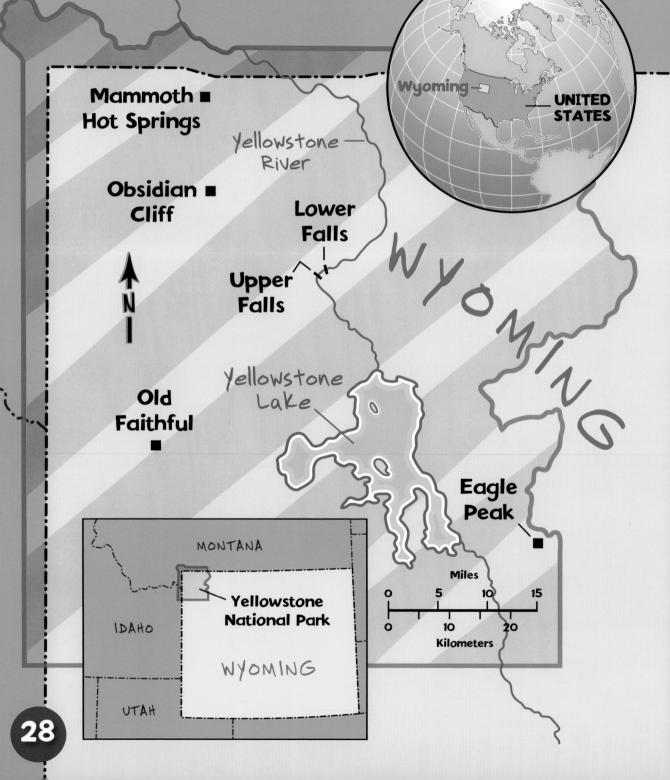

Wyoming

UNITED STATES

Mammoth ■
Hot Springs

Yellowstone River

Obsidian ■
Cliff

Lower Falls

N

Upper Falls

WYOMING

Yellowstone Lake

Old Faithful ■

Eagle Peak ■

MONTANA

Yellowstone National Park

IDAHO

WYOMING

UTAH

Miles
0   5   10   15

0   10   20
Kilometers

Fun Facts

- Yellowstone's winters are cold and snowy. Most of the roads are closed. Visitors ride snowmobiles, ski, ice-skate, and snowshoe.

- Yellowstone gets its name from the yellow cliffs near the park.

- Early explorers to Yellowstone came home with amazing stories of boiling pools and fountains of hot water. Some said they could cook a fish in a stream. Many people thought the stories were made up!

- Yellowstone's volcano is still active. But scientists do not expect it to erupt soon.

- Yellowstone has more than three hundred geysers.

Glossary

erupt: to burst or blow up

geyser: a natural fountain of hot water and steam

glacier: a huge sheet of ice that moves slowly over land

hot spring: a stream with hot, steamy water

lava: very hot melted rock that comes out of a volcano

national park: a protected natural area. The U.S. government runs national parks.

volcano: an opening in Earth's surface through which hot ash, lava, and rock shoot up

Further Reading

Kalman, Bobbie. *Yellowstone National Park*. New York: Crabtree, 2010.

Old Faithful Geyser Live!
http://www.nps.gov/yell/photosmultimedia/yellowstonelive.htm

Walker, Sally M. *Glaciers*. Minneapolis: Lerner Publications Company, 2008.

Walker, Sally M. *Volcanoes*. Minneapolis: Lerner Publications Company, 2008.

Yellowstone National Park—for Kids
http://www.nps.gov/yell/forkids/index.htm

Yellowstone National Park Photos
http://travel.nationalgeographic.com/places/gallery/yellowstone_great-fountain-geyser.html

Index

animals, 4, 15, 22, 24–25

Colter, John, 13

Eagle Peak, 21

geysers, 10, 16, 26
glaciers, 11
Grand Canyon, 20

hot springs, 9–10, 17, 26

Mammoth Hot Springs, 17, 28
mountains, 8, 21

Native Americans, 12

Obsidian Cliff, 19, 28
Old Faithful, 16, 28

stone trees, 18, 26

volcano, 7–8, 19

Wyoming, 6, 28

Yellowstone River, 20, 28

Photo Acknowledgments

The images in this book are used with the permission of: © Flip Chalfant/The Image Bank/Getty Images, p. 4; © Darrell Gulin/The Image Bank/Getty Images, p. 5; © Richard Broadwell/Alamy, p. 6; © Carsten Peter/National Geographic/Getty Images, p. 7; © Klaus Nigge/National Geographic/Getty Images, p. 8; © Annie Griffiths Belt/CORBIS, p. 9; © O. Louis Mazzatenta/National Geographic/Getty Images, p. 10; © Arctic-Images/Iconica/Getty Images, p. 11; © Gerad Smith, p. 12; © Macduff Everton/CORBIS, p. 13; Library of Congress (LC-USZ62-100949), p. 14; © Karlene Schwartz, pp. 15, 19 (both); © Karl Weatherly/Photodisc/Getty Images, p. 16; © Julian Pottage/Robert Harding World Imagery/Getty Images, p. 17; © Wolfgang Kaehler/Alamy, p. 18; © Eastcott Momatiuk/Riser/Getty Images, p. 20; courtesy National Park Service, p. 21; © phil gould/Alamy, p. 22; © Willard Clay/Photolibrary/Getty Images, p. 23; © Jonathan Blair/CORBIS, p. 24; © Jeff Foott/Discovery Channel Images/Getty Images, pp. 25, 31; © Adam Jones/The Image Bank/Getty Images, pp. 26–27; Laura Westlund/Independent Picture Service, p. 28; © Ted Wood/Riser/Getty Images, p. 30.

Front cover: © Michele Falzone/Photographer's Choice/Getty Images.